INTERMEDIATE GUIDE TO
NEEDLE FELTING

CW00821478

ARI YOSHINOBU

Table of Contents

Time to Get Ready

Congrats on your completion of the beginner's guide, and welcome to the very first stages of completing your intermediate guide! It makes me so happy to see you here with me again. We have come a long way together, and I hope you are as excited to jump into this new guide as much as I am!

One of the best parts about learning needle felting is that there is never a shortage of things to learn. This is what I love most about this skill and art form; yes, before you ask, it is an art form. I hope that you view your work as art too. A lot of hard work and technical skill goes into making each little creature or figure; those ideas are the very foundation of what art means. There is a lot of destruction in the world: to make something and put it forth into the world is truly special. I hope that you see how much good creative expression does for you and for everyone else around you.

Before we jump into new material, how about we take a moment to review what we learned in the beginner's guide. Since we covered so much in the first guide, it is good to take this moment to refresh what you know before we jump into new projects.

In the beginner's guide, we learned what needle felting is and how the basic principle is relatively simple. All you need to complete a basic structure is a piece of wool and a barbed needle. However, we do not want to stick to making basic structures all the time, do we?

After that, we jumped into the necessary tools needed to complete a felted figure. We mentioned wool and a barbed needle already; the last tool needed is a surface to felt on.

Now, let us test your memory. There are four different types of felting needles: can you name them? Try your best to name them here, and I will include the answers at the end of this section. No peeking!

We also reviewed the different types of wool available. What is your favorite wool that you have used so far? Which wool are you most excited to try out? I love how each wool lends a different texture and feel to each new project. Even if you make the same shape over and over again, using different yarns will result in different products. How fun is that?

Finally, we jumped into some super cute projects together. What was your favorite project that we completed together? Are there any projects that you skipped over? If so, I greatly encourage you to go back and try whichever task you skipped. Did you struggle with any projects or techniques in a task? Again, I strongly encourage you to go back and try them again. As I'm sure you know, practice makes perfect. Each of the projects listed in the beginner's guide are made to teach you vital skills that will help you improve your needle felting projects. By going back and trying difficult techniques or structures multiple times, you are building a stronger understanding and will help you build a stronger technique. Naturally, and over time, you will get better and your hard work will pay off; that is the whole reason you are here in this intermediate guide, right?

Now that we have reviewed the information we learned in the beginner's guide, let us now get to learning new skills! In this guide, we will learn how to make some advanced shapes and work toward making realistic figures. Here, we are going to focus on super cute animal projects with a few that we can alter to reach peak cuteness!

As in the beginner's guide, each of these projects were carefully selected to help you improve your skills. These projects build on the foundation that you formed in the beginner's guide and introduce you to new techniques, new wool fibers, and even a few new tools! I have also included a hand section of tips, tricks, and advice for you to check out. Keep this section close by as I will make references to it during the individual projects. These tips, tricks, and advice are not 'one size fits all': these are things that work great for some people but may not work the best for everyone. I encourage you to at least try them out and modify the suggestions in a way that feels natural to you.

If your goal is to focus on more realistic figures, I included photos of the real animals in natural colors and settings to give you an immediate reference. This will save you the trouble of having to do an Internet search to see what an ermine looks like and then fall into an Internet hole after you discover how cute their little faces are and completely ignore your needle felting project. We do not want this, so I made it simple for you to help you along your journey.

If you are still feeling a little weak on your feet in regard to your needle felting ability, I encourage you to start out by making the projects as they are written. Having that step-by-step instruction to keep flipping back to will help you gain confidence in your abilities. Once you feel more confident, try out some of the tips and tricks in the projects, or alter the instructions slightly to create a figure that is truly your own.

That being said, there are opportunities to take all of these projects a step further. At the end of each project, I list some ideas of how you can modify the figures to create different and related creatures. These are just suggestions—you by no means have to follow them. They are there just to spark your creativity and encourage you to think about projects in different ways. I hope you like the ideas, and I hope they help you think of other ways that you can use these projects to create even more projects! If you think of ideas, feel free to jot them down so that you do not forget them later on.

Most importantly, as you start to dive into these projects, take your time going through them. Learning how to needle felt is a marathon, not a sprint. If you rush through all of the projects, you are going to make mistakes and break a few needles, which will lead to frustration. Rushing is not necessary, and frustration is certainly not ideal. Slow and steady practice is much more relaxing and enjoyable! Take your time and enjoy making nine new little creatures!

Take a moment right now to flip back to the table of contents. Check out the projects that are available to you in this book. What are you most excited to make? Are there any projects that you are hesitant about? Do your best to try out each project at least once: I guarantee that you will learn something new and have lots of fun doing it.

Let us raise our needles to the beginning of your new journey to becoming a pro in needle felting—just watch out for that pointy end! We would not want any injuries before you start creating any projects.

*Four types of needles: triangle, star, twisted/spiral, and reverse. Did you get any of them? All four? Look at you go, you rockstar!

Chapter 1:

Needle Felting Tips and Tricks

Needle felting is an art that should be truly admired. It takes great patience and hard work to make the beautiful figures that you see all across the Internet. Thankfully, the art of needle felting has grown in popularity in the past few years. This is good news for beginners or ones at the intermediate level because you have so many tools and tricks literally at your fingertips. In the beginner's guide, you learned a lot of important skills and information, but there is always room for improvement. Collecting advice—like in this next section and on the Internet in guides and tutorials—will help you keep reaching and achieving your goals. Seeking out this information will also help motivate you to reach for higher goals as you grow. I hope that these nine little projects make your fingers itch with creative energy and encourage you to seek new projects beyond what is in this guide. With so many adorable projects out there, who would not want to try to get better?

As we discussed before, there is always something new to learn during your needle felting journey. In this chapter, I have compiled a group of tips and tricks to help your journey from beginner to expert go smoothly. Some of these are best practices that will help you successfully master a skill; others are suggestions that people have found to work well for them. Take each tip as a tip. You by no means have to follow any of these ideas. All I ask of you is that you take a few moments to try out the suggestions when you are completing projects. If you never try them, how will you know if you like them or not?

No matter what, I hope you come away from this chapter with new knowledge and armed with techniques that will help you reach the next level in your needle felting journey.

Time to dig in!

Tips, Tricks, and Advice

Before Felting

1. When you have a small piece of wool, before starting, rub the wool between your hands. This will help to bring the individual fibers together and help you get a head start on your felting.

2. When you have medium or large sheets of wool, keep them in their sheet formation. This saves you the headache—and extra work—of smoothing out unnecessary bumps later on. Trust me: you will thank me for this tip later.

3. It is always best to start small: with wool, that is. If you are unsure of the amount of wool that you may need to start a project, start off with a small amount, then add as needed. You can always add wool to a project, but you cannot take it away; you would not want your elephant head turning into a rock hard boulder, would you?

4. When a project calls for a large, round piece, you can save on wool and time by starting with balls of acrylic or polyfill. You can either gather the acrylic together and begin felting it into a sphere, then cover it in wool or take polyfill and wrap thin yarn or thread all around it to create a dense ball, covering with wool once again. This is a great way to save money on wool and cut corners in a larger project that will not disrupt the end result of your project.

5. In a similar suggestion, when creating larger round shapes, you can start by tying a knot or two in the center of your shape: this will help you form a firm core and help you complete a round shape faster.

6. Your needles are going to break: it is inevitable. Felting needles are naturally fragile. It is an excellent practice to keep extra needles nearby when you are starting or working on a project. That way, when one inevitably breaks, you can pick up a new needle and keep going. You do not want anything disrupting your flow once you find it!

7. It is a good habit when starting a project—particularly if it comes in a kit with a limited wool supply—to set aside a little bit of each type or color of wool. This way, when you have completed the project, you can use the wool that you set aside to fix any imperfections or mistakes.

8. If you can, invest in some stencils or cookie cutters to use as guides for small projects. This only works for small flat shapes but greatly helps you form and shape your desired piece. Take your cookie cutter or stencil and stuff it with wool, then begin poking. Keep the wool within the stencil and flip it over to begin poking the other side. Do

this poke, flip, poke dance until the wool becomes firm and is in the shape that you desire. When the wool has taken shape, focus on cleaning up the edges. Only remove the stencil or cutter when you are confident that the wool will hold its shape.

9. No one wants sore fingers: get in the good habit of holding your wool so that you can see your fingers at all times. Move slowly and carefully when you begin to poke to avoid hitting your fingers.

During Felting

1. Patience is key when starting a new project. When you pick up a new piece of wool, it can be hard to see how a soft and fluffy piece can turn into a dense shape of your desire. Be patient and begin to poke. Only after approximately 5-10 minutes will you start to see the wool firm up. The more you poke, the more the fibers will get tangled up together and the smaller your wool will become. It is important not to rush this stage. Take your time when forming your shapes. Rushing to get soft wool to become dense will just result in broken needles and broken spirits. Think of it like a smooth rhythm.

2. Consider investing in a needle felting pen. A needle felting pen allows you to use multiple needles at one time versus a single needle. Naturally, this does speed up your process dramatically. Of course, this is not a necessary investment but it will save you time. There are many styles available at your local and online craft stores. I encourage you to check them out even just to see how they work. Consider watching a few videos first to see if this tool is something you are interested in.

3. Pull the needle out in the same direction that you put it in. This is perhaps the most important tip of all, so it bears repeating. Pull the needle out in the exact same direction that you intend to put it in! It is not about pressure, but straight/precise angles. When you push a needle in and bring it out at a different angle, you will most likely break the needle. Not only is this a headache because it stalls your progress, when you unnecessarily break a needle it can be dangerous. You can poke yourself or lose half of the needle for someone else to poke themselves later on. If you do break a needle, as everyone eventually does, be sure to keep track of the pieces and promptly remove or dispose of them to save yourself from injury.

4. Do not force the needle into the wool. Again, needle felting is not about pressure but precise and straight angles. You will break your needles if you force it into the wool. As shapes become denser, move slower. This will not only help you stay uniform, it will also help you avoid breaking needles.

5. What do you do if you break a needle? Think of this as a large splinter. Gently squeeze the wool to expose the broken needle inside your shape. Be careful not to put your fingers in the spot where the needle is. Find some tweezers and carefully, yet firmly remove the needle from the shape. Try not to pull it at a wrong angle, just like when you are working. Another option to remove a broken needle from inside a wool piece is to find scissors and make small cuts around the area where the needle disappeared. Remember when we were smart and saved little pieces of wool before we started our project? This is the perfect time to break out a piece to patch up the hole

that you just cut into your project. Felt the loose pieces of wool into the hole to close it up.

6. For round objects, uniformity is key. Do not poke in one place repeatedly. Instead, move around your shape in a uniform way and poke randomly but evenly. When creating round objects, you should move the figure with almost every poke to ensure that you are poking all around. If you do not move the sphere around and only poke in one area, you will not be creating a round sphere, but you will be creating unwanted dimples and shapes. Think about it: if with every poke the wool gets denser and smaller, then poking in one area 10 times but in another area only two times will result in a lopsided sphere.

7. Small pieces can be difficult to attach to larger pieces. A pro tip is to leave some loose wool on your pieces at the exact place that you will later attach the pieces together. Visualize cotton candy here. You will have a dense shape with wispy or fluffy pieces on the ends. A further pro tip: try not to eat the wool. Unfortunately, it is not actually cotton candy. Anyone hungry for some sugar right now?

8. In some projects, you may desire to use plastic pieces for eyes or noses. A great tip is to mark the spot where you want to attach the plastic piece with a needle. Then, find your trusty scissors and make a small cut in that exact area. Find some glue and add it to your plastic piece. Promptly insert the plastic piece into the hole. I like to hold the piece for a few seconds to make sure the glue gets all up in the wool before it dries.

9. If you find yourself adding a new and fluffy piece of wool onto an almost completed shape—maybe you are filling

a hole from a broken needle or you are adding wool to make the shape bigger—do not poke too hard. If you do, your shape will become distorted; no one wants a distorted wolf body, do we?

10. You will know when a shape is almost complete when the piece begins to firm up and become difficult to poke. When you get to this point, do a little happy dance to celebrate your new shape!

Finishing Up

1. If you complete your shape only to find little gaps left in your final project, you can try rolling small balls of wool between your fingers. Insert and put felt on these small balls into the gaps in your shape to fill them up.

2. If you complete your shape and find that you are not happy with the end result, feel free to lift up the wool with your needle (gently, of course). Only pick up the top layers of wool here. Add some of the extra wool that you smartly set aside at the beginning of the project to fill in the gaps that you just created and redo the shape or redo the details that you are unhappy with.

3. If you are making small details with wool—particularly in faces—be sure not to use too much wool at the beginning. This is an area that people often start with way too much and then have bulky features. If you do this, it is okay. Chalk it up to a learning experience and remember to use less next time. Like we have said before, it is easier to add wool to enhance features than it is to remove wool.

Tools

When you are just starting out, you do not need a ton of equipment to make figures. However, there are some tools and accessories that can make needle felting easier or even help make your techniques neater and better. Here are some tools that are not necessary but that you might want to invest in at some point in your needle felting journey.

1. Needle felting needles. If you are here, chances are you already have one or two needles. As you continue to learn, it is good to start building up your needle collection. Invest in getting different sized needles and back up needles for when your main needles inevitably break. They are going to break: a lot. Even when you are an expert. Felting needles come in many sizes from strong to thin. Each needle has a different effect and will produce a different end result. It is recommended that you have at least a strong and thin needle to do both binding and detail work. As you can assume, a strong needle is harsher and helps you firm up the shapes that you want to make. Whereas the thin needle helps you smooth out the shapes that you have made and add small delicate details, like facial features.

2. Needle felting pen. This tool allows you to hold multiple needles at the same time. This helps you create shapes in almost half the time of a single needle. Just think about it: instead of one single needle poking in one area at a time, a pen allows you to make multiple pokes in multiple areas at the same time. Sounds pretty great, right? Do some Internet searches or check out your local craft store to find what is available to you. These are typically not very expensive, and in my opinion, a good tool to add to your belt.

3. Felting thimbles. Yes! Felting thimbles exist. I am sure by now you have poked yourself at least once or twice. If you have, you know how terribly painful this can be. Felting needles help you protect your precious fingers. I mean, how can you create figures if your fingers are too sore? Felting thimbles do not seem to be too popular in the mainstream felting community. Where I have noticed people who use them absolutely love them. The ones I have seen have been made out of a thick leather which protects your fingers in a stylish way! The thick leather is great, because it is extremely difficult to puncture at the pressure level that you should be needle felting. Remember, pressure is not important when felting but instead accurate and straight pokes.

4. Sharp scissors. Most people have at least one set of scissors in their house already, but chances are, these scissors are multi-functional. If you use your household scissors to cut everything under the sun, chances are they might be kind of dull. Think about investing in a sharp pair that is just for your needle felting figures. If you do this, look for a small pair with sharp ends. This will help you make precise cuts like with eye and nose attachments.

5. Felting mat. Chances are that you already have some version of this tool, but there are lots of types of mats out there! Do some research to see what types are available to you and consider trying out a few. There are bristled mats, common foam mats, sponge foam mats, or homemade pin cushion type mats. Be like Goldilocks and figure out which type of mat is just okay and which type of mat is just right for you.

6. Zullitool. In some of the projects in this guide, the materials list calls for what is called a Zullitool. This is a cool new tool that is super helpful to make a variety of shapes. The tool itself looks almost like a wooden wand, which is a fitting description for something that is so magical. This tool has two sides: a flat one inch side and a small skewer on the other side. Both of these ends are used to wrap wool around to create body shapes versus felting a flat piece of wool into a 3-D shape. This is great for smaller projects and it helps you save wool. Later in the mouse tutorial, we will put this tool to use. I will also talk about alternatives that you can use if you do not want to buy a Zullitool right off the bat. These alternatives are a great way to try out a similar technique and see if you like it.

Like I said, you do not need a lot of tools to complete even complicated figures. This is good news if you do not wish to buy a lot of extra tools or would not want to spend the extra money. Of course, I am not suggesting or expecting you to go out and buy these tools all in one go. If you do want to purchase some, consider buying only what you need when you need it or per new project. This is a cost effective way to add versatile tools to your toolbelt without breaking the bank.

Important Advice to Remember

1. Practice, practice, practice. The only way you are going to get better at needle felting is to practice. When you are learning, it is good to set aside time every week to work on a project. Now, I am not asking you to set aside 30 hours a week to pure needle felting practice: we need to be realistic. However, when you set time aside every week to intentionally practice felting, you are

committing to learning the practice. Every minute that you put into this skill will pay off down the line. Before you know it, you will be a needle felting rockstar!

2. When you get into a practice rhythm, create a little ritual around your practice. You have already carved out this time, now use it as a moment of self-care. Put on your favorite album, show, or movie. Pour yourself a cup of your favorite hot drink—pro tip: hot chocolate and needle felting go hand in hand—or even burn a new candle. Whatever you enjoy or whatever relaxes you, combine it with your needle felting practice. This will help you create a relaxing flow; if you get frustrated at a technique or structure, then you can pause for a moment, take a few deep breaths, or a few sips of your hot drink and reset. Use this moment to take stock of what you are doing and what is making you frustrated and fix it.

3. Finally, and perhaps most importantly, never compare yourself to other needle felting artists. I know that it is instinct to see examples of experts doing incredible things with wool and you think to yourself that you will never be able to do that. Trust in the practice, trust in the time and effort that you put in, and trust in yourself. You are not going to be an expert right away. Everyone finds their own groove in their own time. Let yourself get there because you will with time and practice. Everyone started out as a beginner/novice just like you, too. Remember, every "imperfection" is not an "imperfection" but what makes the figure uniquely yours. You can have a group of a hundred people follow the same instructions, and guaranteed, every single figure will look differently. This is what makes the art of needle felting! Take ownership of your figures, even your

very first ones. Just try not to get all Dr. Frankenstein on me!

Final Thoughts on Tips, Tricks, and Advice

What tips and tricks did you enjoy the most? Have you discovered any of these in one of your beginner-style projects? Which tip or trick are you most excited to employ in your next needle felting project?

As you will come to find out, what works for one person may not work for another. Keep an open mind when you approach projects, and try out new things until you figure out just what works for you. I also encourage you to find other people that are interested in needle felting. Finding a person or a community is a great way to expand your knowledge, work on your skills, and meet some pretty cool people along the way! You can start by checking out blogs or videos on the Internet. With an expanding interest in needle felting in the craft world, felting blogs are growing, too. Do some quick searches and see what is out there. If you do not feel comfortable jumping into conversations, then just take a back seat and see what other people in this community are doing. As you get to know what is out there, start adding comments to various projects. Ask questions about something that you are unsure of, and be sure to tell them how much you enjoyed their material. Everyone needs some positivity and encouragement in their lives; be a source of light!

Now, who is ready to dive into their next needle felting project?

Chapter 2:

Wandering Wolf

Both feared and revered, wolves have been a part of human history and storytelling for as long as people have been around. In western culture, the story of Little Red Riding Hood probably comes to mind first or maybe even the story of the Three Little Pigs. If you are a fan of wolves, you might find these stories to be degrading toward wolves. If you are fearful of wolves, then maybe you think that these stories are just right. Whatever you think, these stories showcase one important trait about wolves: how smart and foreboding they can be.

These stories were created out of sheer human instinct for survival. Wolves were notorious for preying on and killing livestock that were vital to feeding the human population. So, if wolves were the bad guys in stories, then they became the bad guys in real life and their removal would not seem like such a bad idea. This idea reigns supreme in communities that relied on farming to survive. In communities that relied on hunting, the image of a wolf was entirely different. It is no wonder human communities that relied on hunting would admire and even attempt to mimic wolf hunting patterns.

Nowadays, wolves rarely come in contact with most humans. This is mainly out of this century and the long fear of being hunted by humans. In most areas, the wolf population is relatively low—especially compared to the human population—which means that wolves and humans live entirely separate from each other. This is good for wolves and humans alike but perhaps not so good for human storytelling; however, that is still okay: humans have never run out of bad guys to put in their stories.

The gray wolf is the largest and most common of the wolf species. From this, there are a handful of subspecies that exist (think coyotes, dingoes, jackals, hyenas, and even the domestic dog). These subspecies are so closely related that hybrid species are possible, although dangerous if domesticated.

Wolves also live in strong communities on which they depend upon for food and survival. If you have a few minutes, check out some videos of wolves hunting. Their strategy is incredible and very captivating to watch!

The fur of a wolf is typically mottled and common colors include white, brown, gray, and black. Although wolves appear to be mostly one color, it is a combination of these four colors that make up the appearance of a single solid coloration. This effect makes this project extremely unique. If you are looking for a more streamlined project the first time around, you can make an all white, brown, or black wolf because they do exist in nature. If you are looking to try out some new skills, I encourage you to try at least a mix of two colors to make up the wolf's fur or even try all three if you are very adventurous.

Do not forget that the ears and muzzle of a wolf have a slightly pointed style and the tail is nice and fluffy.

There is nothing to fear about this first project. In fact, this little figure is far more adorable and playful than menacing and definitely deserves a spot on your shelf next to your other projects. Now, all you have to do is get to making this little guy or gal!

Wolf Instructions

Materials

- Metal wife for skeleton

- Felting needles

- Felting pad

- Wolf spunk

- Black, natural color, and brown roving

Steps

1. Grab your metal wire. For this step, you can either cut the wire to the size that you would like or you can leave it attached and cut it after you have created your wire skeleton.

2. Make a rough skeleton of the wolf with the wire. Start with the head by adding a slight bend to the wire. Bend the wire again to create the distinction between the neck and the body. From here, mark out the length that you want your back to be and snip off the wire. Twist extra wire evenly on top of the head, neck, and back end to create a stronger structure. Add wire in a v-shape to the front and back to create the legs. Make sure to wrap these wires together to strengthen again. Finally, add some curves to the legs (particularly in the hind legs because they have the most natural curve), including bends for the feet here as well. Add wire to any section that feels particularly weak. Think about the head, neck, and legs that are going to hold the most weight.

3. Take natural color felt and wrap tightly around the skeleton to form a base. We wrap a layer tightly at first to build a good base that we can next felt onto it to keep building up the body.

4. Add more layers to keep building up the body. By this point, you should be able to needle felt to tighten the wool and hold it in place.

5. Now, start slowly adding layers on it to give it a proper mass.

6. Add detail figures to it like paws, a tail, etc.

7. After that, use black felt to make eyes and a nose on the face of the wolf.

8. Mix some natural color and brown felt together to create that fun branded, or varied, fur that is very common in wolves.

9. Add it on the sculpture to add details of the wolf.

10. Now, needle felt the ears of the wolf using the same mixed felt. Make sure to create a slightly curved shape to the ears. You cannot send you wolf out into the world not being able to hear properly!

11. Add more details to the body of the wolf with the help of the wolf spunk.

12. Add details to the tail and use multiple needles for better results. The multiple needles with help create a fluffy tail. Follow the natural curve of a wolf's tail by adding fluff as it gets farther away from the body then coming to almost a point at the end.

13. At last, take some black felt and add details to the paw and needed areas.

Now your wolf is ready to hunt.

Pro-tip:

Want to take this project a step further and truly unlock your felting skills? Consider using this shape to create some of the subspecies of the gray wolf. Do some image research to find examples of coyotes, dingoes, and different types of wolves based on location like the Italian wolf, Indian plains wolf, red wolf, etc. Alter the size and slight shape based on the new species of your choice. This is also a fun way to experiment with different colors and facial features (for example, dingos have a more dog-shaped face whereas coyotes closely resemble wolves apart from size).

You can also create domestic dogs from this tutorial. Of course, larger breeds of dogs work best when translating this tutorial over to a dog. You can attempt to make smaller breeds by starting out with a smaller wire skeleton and making your shapes based on the look of a breed. Get creative, and try out a few options.

Try out as many ideas as you would like: the options are literally endless!

Chapter 3:

Al-Pac-a My Wool

Alpacas and llamas. What really is the difference between these two animals? Is there even an important enough distinction between these two animals?

Although these two animals closely resemble each other, there are differences between them. Let us review a few to give you a good idea before jumping into the project. Both animals are native to South America and their coats can be harvested for wool/fleece. One stark difference between the two animals is that alpacas are significantly smaller than llamas. Also, llamas are bred and raised to be working animals whereas alpacas are bred specifically for their fleece. A common misconception about llamas and alpacas is that they often spit at humans. It seems as if the spitting is the only fact that people know about these two animals. In reality, both of these animals are unlikely to spit at humans. Spitting is a defense mechanism usually reserved for others of their own kind. Do they still occasionally spit at humans? Sure: it really is not that great. Camels have a similar response and it is just their way of saying that they are uncomfortable in whatever situation they are currently in. You cannot really get mad at them for communicating in the only way they know how, can you? I guess it all depends on whether or not you have just been spit on.

Alpacas are very intelligent animals and are extremely cute which makes them a perfect candidate to turn into a felted figure. They live in herds and are very playful and social. I think that is one thing that makes people love alpacas so much. I mean, have you ever seen a video of alpacas hopping around? Try not to look up videos unless you are prepared for a cuteness overload.

In this chapter, we will be creating a lovely little alpaca together. This project is great for intermediate felties because you can experiment with different colors and types of wool for this project.

Want to elevate your alpaca figurine to the next level? Consider using actual alpaca fleece! As I am sure you know by now, sheep's wool tends to be slightly coarse, especially compared to alpaca fleece. When you try out alpaca fleece for the first time, you will be stunned by how luxurious it is. Also, it is hypoallergenic which makes it a perfect alternative for people who are sensitive to natural sheep's wool. Plus, everyone that sees your little figure will be so impressed that you used real alpaca fur.

What is also exciting about this alpaca project is that it is great for trying out new and natural colors. Alpacas come in a variety of browns and whites, and most animals tend to be one solid color. This means that you never have to worry about trying to blend different body colors in this project. In the instructions below, the wool required for this project is listed as "natural color," so the choice is yours. Will you make a brown, tan, or white alpaca? Here in this photo, this little alpaca is a lovely tan color.

24

If you are not super familiar with the look of an alpaca, take some time to observe this picture below. Notice how the ears are rather pointed and sit higher up on the head than other animals. Also pay attention to how the legs are shaped. The body is lush and full of fleece whereas the legs taper down the hooves. From the side, alpaca's necks are very curved in the front but more angular in the back where they meet the body. Their hind legs have a natural curve, much like dogs. The natural curve of the hind legs meets a round belly. Finally, and perhaps most importantly, alpaca's tails sit close to the body and flop over in one glorious clump of fleece. If you are unsure of shapes, do a few more image searches to see different angles.

Alpaca Instructions

Materials

- Felting needles

- Felting pad

- Natural color (of your choice) and black roving

- Multi-needle holder

Steps

1. First, take out a large amount of natural color felt.

2. Divide it into three small strands (for the ears, nose, and tail), four long, slightly bigger, low density strands (for legs), one medium size strand (for the head), and one huge strand (for the body).

Pro-tip: When dividing and setting aside these pieces, it might be extremely helpful to label them. An easy way to do this is to find some sticky notes: write a quick note about which body part goes with which sticky note. With moving parts like this, it is extremely helpful to I.D. them at this stage of the game versus struggling to remember them when you are in the middle of the project. Do not worry if you have to set them aside with a sticky note; it is really hard to remember when you are trying to focus on the instructions!

3. Take one of the four long strands and give it a shape of an alpaca leg. These should be standard cylinders with curved bottoms for the feet. Remember from the photo that the legs taper down toward the hooves, especially

with the fleece. Without the fleece, an alpaca's legs are rather skinny but still slightly curved.

4. Add toes to it: three should do.

5. Repeat above steps three more times to create three more legs of equal size and shape. Do not forget to mimic the natural shape of the hind legs. This is important to achieving a realistic creature versus a round body on stick legs.

Pro-tip: When making these individual pieces, remember to leave the one end loose for easy attachment later on.

6. Grab the small pieces of wool that you set aside for the nose, tail, and ears. For the ears, create rounded triangles. Create an indented center to give the ears a nice shape. The nose should closely resemble a rounded rectangle. If it is boxy, do not worry about it at this point: we will enhance its shape later on. Finally, the tail should be oval in shape on one end. Leave the other end loose to attach to the body. Be sure to hold up these pieces to your alpaca's body when you make it in the next step. Adjust your shapes when needed.

7. Now find the huge strand that you set aside.

8. Place it on the felting pad and give it the shape of an alpaca's belly. This should be a pretty standard rectangle at this stage. We will enhance the shape later on. Be sure to rotate it regularly to create an even shape.

9. Now find the medium strand that you set aside.

10. Give it the shape of an alpaca's head and neck. This shape will be one long cylinder. Do not curve the top for the

head, we will add dimension to the face later with other pieces.

11. Attach the neck/head to the body.

12. Now take some more felt and loosen its strands. Tear apart sections until you have thin wool that you can see through.

13. Use these loose strands of thread to make all of those body parts puffier. Use multiple needles with the needle holder if you feel it is necessary. Remember that a needle holder or pen will help you move faster through this step, but a single needle will do the job just fine if that is all that you have available to you. If you are looking to make a smoother figure at this stage, be sure to use a thinner needle to smooth out the bumps and fill in any gaps or holes that might be lurking around. Make sure to cover the entire body and to add a nice round shape to the underbelly. The top of the alpaca's back should be relatively straight in comparison. If you want to get really realistic, encourage a neat angle where the neck meets the body.

14. Find the ears and nose and attach them to the head.

15. Take some more of the loose felt and use only one needle for this task. Add this loose felt around the nose and face to create a fluffier shape. Make sure to save room for the eyes. If you look at the photo of the alpaca again, notice that the fleece above the eyes is heavy and almost creates a hood. Whereas there is no extra fleece present around the nose. You can add extra fleece to the nose or muzzle area if you desire to create a really fluffy and even shape or you can leave it alone to add more dimension to your alpaca's face.

16. Find your legs and wrap loose wool around each one. Using just one needle again, felt the loose wool in place to keep the fluffiness going. Use a thin needle here again to avoid having any large or rough bumps. Be sure that you do not cover the very end of the feet to ensure that you have a traditionally tapered look.

17. Carefully attach the legs to the body with loose wool. Make sure that there is not a division between the body and the legs. If there are any holes, fill them in with loose wool.

18. Attach the tail and fluff out the body once more.

19. At last, use black felt to add details like the eyes and mouth. The eyes should be simple and round while the mouth should be a typical fish hook shape.

Your alpaca is ready for packing!

Pro-tip:

Now that you know the difference between alpacas and llamas, consider changing this shape to resemble a working llama. Here, you can keep experimenting with mixed colors in a figure (llamas commonly have slight color differences in their coats versus solid alpacas).

In addition to this, consider experimenting with accessories. Because they are bred to be working animals, llamas typically have harnesses, blankets, and packs attached to them. Do some image research and never try to skimp on color! Also, be sure to adjust the shape slightly. Remember that alpacas are smaller than llamas.

Most of these projects in this intermediate guide are geared toward making realistic figures. However, this project is also a great opportunity for you to make an unusual figure. If you are feeling adventurous, try out some wacky colors—think blue, purple, or green!—to switch things up. If you do this, feel free to make its facial features more cartoonish. Add accessories like a hat or a bow. Also, try not to forget adding some blushed cheeks or eyelashes to reach peak cuteness!

Chapter 4:

Isabelle From Animal Crossing

Pop culture enthusiasts and gamers rejoice! Next up in our project list is Isabelle from the popular Animal Crossing: New Horizons game. This project is a great change of pace from the realistic animals that we have been creating so far. Isabelle will also test your needle felting skills because she has a distinct look and style. Try your best to follow the instructions to a T to create an authentic-style Isabelle.

Isabelle Instructions

Materials

- Felting wool (oranges, pale yellow, red, white, green, and blue)

- Felting mat

- Felting needle

- Scissors

- Glue

- Jewelry cutter

- Head pins

- Gloss varnish

- Black polymer clay

Steps

1. We will start by making the head.

2. Use natural color felt (Isabelle is a light shade of yellow) and multiple needles to make a head. Begin with a typical sphere while leaving a section less felted as the whole head. This section needs to be slightly felted—it will become Isabelle's snout in the next step.

3. Start sculpting the face shape properly. Begin by poking in a v-shape on top of the area that you saved from the last section. Continuously poke along this v-shaped line that you have started to create dimension in the sphere.

When you are finished with this step, you should have a sphere and a protruding snout.

4. Then, make ears using orange felt. Isabelle's ears are triangular in shape and closely resemble floppy dog ears.

5. Isabelle's ears have two distinct ridges on them. You can create ridges by continuously poking at the same spot. Make sure to form a scalloped edge along the longer part of the ear and stop the ridges about an inch and a half from the bottom. When you are finished with this step, you should have two ears of equal size with three bumps (or scallops) along the bottom. At this point, you should check the ear size against the head size to make sure they fit. Isabelle's ears should fit from the top to the bottom of the head.

6. Now make a fish tail shape on your foam base in the pale yellow wool color. This piece will be used to create Isabelle's bangs, so make sure that the fish tail shape is wide enough to fit across the top of her head. Adjust accordingly.

7. Snip in the edges to create hair strands. Two snips with your sharp scissor about a half an inch should do the trick. This is to make her bangs appear textured when you attach it to Isabelle's forehead. Be sure to felt around the snips to secure the loose wool. You should not have to do too much felting here.

8. Find the two floppy ears that you just made and attach them to the head using loose felt.

9. Add your fishtail bangs. Use your needle to sculpt it properly. Here, you can create a neat parting of her hair

and felt the bangs to the head at the same time. Make sure it is secure.

10. Now create a bun using orange felt. Isabelle's bun sits straight up at the back of her head and resembles a slightly squashed mushroom. Add some dimension to her hair by mixing orange and yellow felt.

11. Find your sharp scissors and cut a small hole on the top of the head right behind where her hair part stops.

12. With the help of loose felt, attach the bun to that exact spot. Push the bun into the hole and fill in the hole with the loose felt.

13. Find a strip of red wool to make a thick hairband. This hairband will be created on the hair versus on your foam base. Add the red hairband to complete the bun. Make sure the red wool reaches all around the bun and touches but does not morph into Isabelle's bangs.

14. Find some thin white wool to use for Isabelle's mouth area. Remember to start with a little wool and gradually increase in layers as needed. Felt the white wool onto the protruding snout for mouth area detailing.

15. Now create some eyes and nose using polymer clay. Roll out a small piece of black clay. Cut this into small strips. Carefully press the strips into eye shapes. In this figure, Isabelle's eyes are closed and have a slight rainbow shape. Then, make a few noses by flattening small balls of black clay.

Pro-tip: Always make more clay pieces than you need, especially for such small pieces as these. This saves you time if they crack while baking or if you break them while assembling. Make lots because accidents do happen!

16. After giving the clay a proper shape, bake them as per package instructions. Once the pieces have hardened, you can pick the best shapes from your collection and save any extra pieces for other projects. Be sure to test the shapes on your Isabelle head now to make sure the proportions and shapes fit her head.

17. Now take golden head pins (typically used for making jewelry) and shorten them with the help of a jewelry cutter.

18. Now with the help of glue—any glue will do—attach the eyes and nose to the head of the pins. Make sure the glue dries completely.

19. Once the glue has dried completely, hold the pins upright in soft clay. Find your gloss varnish and glaze the tops of the eyes and nose. This varnish helps seal the clay and makes the facial features really pop!

20. Once the varnish has dried, poke holes in Isabelle's face where you want the eyes and nose to go. Add glue to the pin and insert them into the face of Isabella. Make sure to clean up any extra glue that might have leaked out before it dries.

21. Create and open the smiling mouth by using thin wisps of red wool. Again, start with very little and add as necessary. Leave a small rectangular shape at the top opening of the mouth for the look of a front tooth. By using thin wisps of red wool, you create a soft pink color much like the inside of a mouth. Go a step further by varying the red color from more vibrant around the curve to soft and pale pink in the middle where her tongue should be. You can even experiment here with 3-D shapes by indenting at the curve of the mouth.

Repeatedly poke the same area within the curve to help it take shape. Take some thin black wool and outline the shape of the mouth.

22. Set the head aside to start working on the body.

23. Sculpt the body using light green felt. Isabelle's body should resemble a triangular cylinder; just make sure that the top is not too pointy.

24. Add details and trimmings with darker green and white wool. In this project, Isabelle wears a green cardigan with two white buttons. You can achieve this look by creating a Y shape along the body. Place small rectangular pockets on either side of the Y. Then, add white wool to the curve of the Y for her undershirt. Take some thin red wool and create a bow on her white undershirt.

25. Create arms and legs. Start by using her pale yellow skin color to make curved arms. Add white wool to the top (think short sleeve) and create a puffed shirt sleeve. Create two plain yellow legs of equal length.

26. Attach arms to the body.

27. Now wrap the legs in blue felt and use needles to felt it in place. This blue wool is used to make a straight skirt for Isabelle. Poke until the blue wool is combined.

28. Attach the legs to the body with loose wool. Make it so that Isabelle appears to be sitting down.

29. Make a tail similar to a fox with yellow and white wool. The yellow wool should be at the thinner end that attaches to Isabelle's body and the white should be larger at the tip to create the illusion of it being fluffy.

30. Attach the tail to the area between her torso and skirt.

31. Felt all around to make sure the figure is smooth.

32. Finally, attach the head to the body with loose wool.

Pro-tip: Push downward when attaching the head to the body to help the pieces stick together well.

33. Now use different felt to add minor details and finishing touches like blushed cheeks for her smiling face!

Your Isabelle is ready to give out some camping fun and assignments!

Chapter 5:

Mighty Lion

I named this next project the mighty lion because lions truly are mighty. They may not be the largest land mammal—I am looking right at you, elephants!—but they sure know how to command respect. I mean, just look at that gaze! So much power and poise in one glance!

The lion used to have a much larger range across the globe, but now is mainly found only in sub-saharan Africa, with one extremely protected subspecies living in India. Like with other protected species of animals, conflicts with humans have disrupted the survival of these beautiful lions. Although there are a limited number of lions left in the wild, their legacy as the king of animals stays strong. How many stories can you name that feature a prominent lion character? Even in the past century, people have continued to revere and uplift the status of lions.

Think back to the first time that you ever saw a lion in person. For most people, this usually occurs at a zoo. For me, I will forever be in awe by how big lions are. Pictures rarely give a good enough idea about how large and powerful lions truly are. Are you ready to see if you can make a figure that will live up to the legacy of the king of all animals? We will find out!

Lions have some distinct characteristics. The most obvious of these is its mane. The mane, in its honey brown color, creates an almost halo effect around a lion's head. Remember that the mane stretches down the neck, onto the shoulder, and even between its front legs. Its body is a lovely sandy color to help it blend into its surroundings. Another distinction of the lion's look is the little tuft of fur on the very end of its tail. Be sure to include a nice array of browns to achieve the look of a lion.

Lion Instructions

Materials

- Felting wool

- Felting needle

- Felting pad

- Artificial eyes

- Glue

Steps

1. Take a natural color wool and start creating the head. Add a rectangular shaped muzzle to the front of the lion's head.

2. When the sculpting of the head of the lion is done, add eyes by making small incisions where you wish to place the eyes with sharp scissors. Add glue to the plastic eyes and place them in the holes that you just created. I like to hold them in place for a few minutes to make sure that the glue begins to dry and hold the eyes in place. If you made the holes too big, you will have trouble at this stage. Be sure to wipe up any glue that might have leaked out before it dries.

3. After that, give highlights to the lion's face like the mouth and nose using black felt. Add some extra dimension to the face by lining around the eyes. Take a look at the picture above as an example. The lion almost looks like it has a great cat eyeliner—maybe that is where the popular cat eye look comes from. Who knew that lions were so fashion forward?

4. Make two round ears and attach them to the head of the lion. A lion's ears sit slightly off on the sides of the head. Try not to put them up too far and turn your lion into an aardvark.

5. Poke the inside of the ears repeatedly to create a slight curve in the ears.

6. Now take some brown felt and loosen it.

7. Add this loose brown felt to the head of the lion.

8. Add more details to it using some varying colors like light brown or a golden honey color.

9. Now add whiskers to the face of the lion using black felt. Be sure to make these very thin and small to mimic real whiskers. Consider adding small tufts of black felt to the inside of the ears to mimic ear hair.

10. After that, use natural color felt and sculpt the body of the lion.

11. Also sculpt four legs and one tail for the lion.

12. Take some loose brown felt and needle felt it on the lion's body, legs, and tail.

13. Now attach the body to the head of the lion with the help of some loose felt.

14. After that, add minor details to the body, using black felt to create paws on the legs.

15. Make a thin tail out of the main body color. Never forget to add that distinct tuft on the end of the tail!

16. Now attach those legs and the tail to the lion's body.

17. Take a huge amount of felt and loosen it.

18. Needle felt it to the figure from the edge of the neck of the lion to create the mane.

19. Use some more dark-shaded felt to add a second layer of mane to give it a more diverse look. Consider adding very small strands of the mixed color like you did on the head to create a dynamic mane color.

20. Now take a very loose strand of felt.

21. Needle felt them on the lion's body at an angle in a backward direction: this will create a very nice hide of the lion.

22. Now, at last, use some colors to add more dynamic details to it.

Your lion is ready for stalking prey in the Serengeti.

Pro-tip:

The lion tends to be a much more advanced figure, which is perfect for elevating your skills! The mane gives you an opportunity to try out some loose wool skills. Consider creating a lioness to pair with your lion. All you have to do is adjust the size and skip over the mane: pretty simple! Now, you can start your very own pride.

Also consider going back to the wolf tutorial to make a spotted hyena. After you make an elephant later on in this book, you will be well on your way to making your very own food chair, but maybe try to not tell the elephant and the hyena!

Chapter 6:

Meek Winter Ermine

An ermine is an interesting little creature and very worthy to make it into your collection of needle felted animals. I mean, if they were good enough for Leonardo da Vinci, then they are good enough for you!

Ermines are native to Northern America, Northern Europe, and Northern Asia. A pretty wide span, right? Fun fact: in the 19th century, ermines were introduced to New Zealand to combat the rising rabbit population, but they ended up destroying the native bird population! Not so meek and little as they seem, are they?

In this project's instructions, we will be making a white ermine. In nature, ermine's coats change color based on their location. In the summer, an ermine has a sandy brown coat with a white belly. An ermine that lives farther north will shed its sandy brown fur to reveal a lovely all-white coat. Its entire body is white except for the very tip of its tail which is black. As you can imagine, this is to match its natural surroundings to help it survive the winter season.

Ermine fur was actually a luxury fur at one time which makes it pretty fitting to turn it into a felted figure! During its winter white, an ermine's coat is dense and silky. In the summer, its sandy brown top is coarser.

As I mentioned, we will be making an all-white ermine here. If you desire, you can make a sandy brown summer ermine. If you decide to do this, create the body parts as listed then add brown wool over the body parts. Check out this photo below to see the divide between the brown and the white sections of this little creature.

Ermine Instructions

Materials

- Felting needles sizes 36 (optional), 38, 40, & 42 (you can go higher if desired)

- Coarse wool roving

- White, black, brown, pink, and red merino wool (will vary depending on what you want to make)

- Natural horse/alpaca hair or clear fishing line for whiskers

- Glass eyes with wire loops

- Pipe cleaners

- Sharp scissors

- Super glue

- Needle and thread

Steps

1. First, make a wire skeleton/armature of your ermine. You can do this with either pipe cleaners or plain wire as we have done in other projects. Be sure to fold in any ends to make sure that the wire does not poke through the wool. Ouch!

2. Cover the head and body in roving wool. Wrap this tightly around the figure (do not do the full leg just yet). Add layers of wool to achieve your desired thickness. Felt the wool into place as you go to make sure that it firms up properly. Use a strong needle at first—36 or 38 will do— until you have a rough shape and your wool stays in place.

3. Move up to a 40 needle when you begin felting a denser body shape. Create denser areas with more layers as needed. Places like the shoulder and backside are where

you should be doing this. Again, try not to add too much bulk to the bottom of the feet right now: just enough to cover the wire. Do not move up to a higher needle because your figure will become too hard to work on if you do.

4. Now start adding some layers of Merino wool in your desired color. Merino wool is great because it is fine and soft. Use thin layers and a 42 needle to felt the wool in place. Be sure to add the Merino wool in the same direction that you added the roving wool to avoid a striped appearance. Ensure that the layers are thin so that they blend in with the roving wool well. Keep adding layers until the roving wool is completely covered. This will take some time and many layers.

5. Now create the tail. The tail has a cool loose look that will really elevate your figure; it also takes some time to make this step. Grab some strips of black merino wool and cut these strips into equal sections. If the sections are not equal, it will create a patched look. Fold the sections in half and felt them onto the coarse roving wool using a 42 needle. Keep felting the sides down and felt from multiple directions to make sure that the loose fur gets secured. You will know when you have completed this step when you can tug on the tail gently and the wool stays in place. Snip any unruly hairs to make sure that your tail is all one length and shape.

6. Sculpt the ears, leaving one end loose. Attach the ears to the head with the loose ends. Felt the ears to secure them. Make sure that the loose ends are felted so that they flow down the back of the neck in one direction.

7. Take your needle and felt repeatedly in the inside of the ears to create a slightly curved shape.

8. Add layers of Merino wool to the head to give it more shape. These layers will also help you create a denser head figure. Do not make the eye area too dense so that you can attach them in the next section. The snout of your ermine should be a nice rounded rectangle and protrude from the skull. The snout should also be firm up the center of the head to create a divot where the eyes will be. Add layers of wool to this center section to create this shape.

9. Add your eyes by cutting a slit and gluing the eyes in place. Make sure to wipe up any excess glue that might leak out before it dries.

10. Next, focus on the feet. Where you did not add much wool? Add a few thin layers or Merino wool to make sure that the pipe cleaner and roving is completely covered. Ermines have petite feet, so make sure that you are not adding too many bulky layers, just enough to cover.

11. Take your pink wool and make little paw pads and toes on the bottom of the feet. These are pretty simple circles and should be made using thin layers of pink wool. Start with very little and keep adding as needed.

12. Here, take your needle and thread to shape the toes. The thread should be the same color as your wool so that it does not stick out. Create four toes by using the thread to pull the wool in. This should look similar to a rounded scallop.

13. Add some very thin layers of pink wool to the inside of the ears.

14. Alternatively, you can also add some acrylic paint to add details to your ermine's face. Add pink to the ears instead of wool. Add some grey tones around the eyes to add dimension and enhance the raised bridge of the nose. Create a nose with a reddish-brown color in the shape of an upside down triangle. Add any other details that you think you would like to create a truly dynamic little creature.

15. Finally, you can add whiskers to your little ermine with natural horse or alpaca hair or with fishing wire. Thread your needle with whatever material you are going to use and push it through the nose in equal distance on both sides. Add at least three whiskers for a realistic look and super glue them in place.

Your ermine is ready to do whatever ermines do.

Pro-tip:

Since ermines have been used in art and were once considered a luxury fur, consider elevating your plain ermine to a fancy ermine. Create a socialite figure, and give this little lad or lass some fun jewelry or even a bow tie and hat! These little accessory details are not only cute, but will also help you branch out and try new and difficult shapes. Also, consider making both a summer and winter ermine!

Chapter 14:

Funky Macaron Garlands

Whether you like to use garlands to decorate for a party, holiday, or other special occasion, you will absolutely love these whimsical macarons that you will thread into a funky garland. You might initially hang them up for a party, but this macaron garland might become a permanent staple in your home decor!

Materials Required

1. Felting Needle

2. Wool roving of different colours (One ounce of roving will make two one-inch macarons, so plan accordingly)

3. White roving yarn

4. Multi felting needle

5. Embroidery needle

6. Baker's Twine

7. Foam base

Steps to Follow

1. Cut a 48-inch long piece of colored wool roving.

2. Spread out the roving a bit to loosen the fibers. It is easier to work with flat roving than a wound up strand.

3. Take the stretched out roving and start to roll it into a tight ball shape.

4. Do not just roll it back and forth, because then the fibers will be very smooth and you will have to needle felt it for a longer period of time. Rolling the ball every which way will start to tangle the fibers before you take a felting needle to it. It does not matter if the ball is lumpy at this point because you will end up needle felting it into a slightly different shape.

5. Move the wool ball to the foam base so you can safely use the needle tool. You can use one or two needles at the same time, or even use a needle felting pen to prick the roving over and over again.

6. As you felt the wool ball, start to shape it into a thick disc that looks like a macaron.

7. While you are working, be sure to turn your work over and prick it with your felting needle from all sides.

8. Once you have a nice macaron shape, cut a 6" length of white roving yarn. Tie the yarn around the center of the macaron so it looks like the cookie's filling.

9. Make sure that the white yarn stays in place while you felt it onto the brightly colored macaron. You can felt this yarn just like you felted the wool into the macaron shape, but you will not have to work as hard. Just slightly felting the white yarn will adhere it to the macaron so it will stay in place.

10. When you have felted the white yarn all the way around the macaron, connect the ends of the white yarn so that it looks like a complete piece (and realistic filling!).

11. Cut the excess yarn off so that it will not hang from the finished product.

12. Repeat steps 1 through 11, using a variety of colors, until you have as many macarons as you would like to add to your garland. Once you make a couple of these sweet treats, you will be able to create them fairly quickly! This type of repetitive task is a great way to polish your needle felting skills.

13. Once you have all of your macarons ready, you can string them onto the garland.

14. Thread the baker's twine through the eye of the embroidery needle. You can actually use any thread to be the string of your garland, but Baker's Twine is sturdy and comes in cute candy colors!

15. Stitch the thread through the top layers of each macaron so the cookies will dangly slightly from the garland. If you want to thread the macarons through the middle, you can, but you might want to tie a knot before and after each macaron to keep it in position.

There is a lot of room for adaptation with this pattern! You can choose to make your macarons in pastel colors to look realistic, or you can use vibrant colors to make them brighten up your room. You can use two or three colors and make a repeating pattern on your garland, or you can use many different colors so that each individual macaron is unique.

Chapter 8:

Elegant Elephant

They spark joy and love for so many people, it is a shame that they are so big; I'm sure many people would love to have an elephant as a pet. After this tutorial, you no longer have to wish!

I am quite sure you have heard all of the facts about elephants. Elephants have an incredible memory, they have a lifespan almost the same as humans, and are so compassionate for such a large animal, it is no wonder people love them. With such distinct features like floppy ears, long tusks and trunks, and thick legs there is no other animal quite as unique as this lovable giant.

You are also probably familiar with the two distinct types of elephants: African and Asian. Although very similar, you can tell them apart by the size of their ears—African elephants have larger ears than their Asian counterparts. For this project, I will leave it up to you to decide which species of elephant you wish to make. When deciding which ear size to go for, remember that the shape of each elephant's ears closely resembles the continent on which they live. Pretty easy to remember!

Elephant Instructions

Materials

- Felting wool (blue, black, and pink)

- Plastic eyes

- Felting needles

- Felting pad

- Metal wire

Steps

1. Start by taking a big chunk of blue wool.

2. Roll it out and start poking it to give it a circular shape.

3. Create one more ball but bigger than the previous one.

4. Now take a small metal wire and fold it in half. Wrap this wire together to strengthen it.

5. Wrap some blue felt around it to make a leg. Roll it very tightly and poke it to shape it firmly.

6. Take a really small amount of pink wool and make the base of the foot.

7. Repeat this process to create four total legs.

8. Now join your head to the body with the help of some loose wool.

9. Now join all four legs of the elephant.

10. Create the trunk of the elephant using the same technique you created the legs.

11. Use a tiny bit of pink wool to create the nostrils at the end of the trunk.

12. Now glue two eyes on the elephant.

13. After that, create the ears of the elephant. The size and shape of these ears depends on what species of elephant you are making.

14. Use pink wool to give finishing touches to the ears.

15. Attach them to the head of the elephant using some loose wool.

16. Now take some black wool and add highlights to the face.

17. Finally, glue a bow/flower to the head.

Your elephant is ready to eat some peanuts!

Pro-tip:

Which elephant did you choose to make? Now that you have made one, why not make the other? I mean, who would want just one elephant when they can have two!

Although elephants appear to be one solid color, their skin is very unique and wrinkly. It folds over in areas to trap water and creates areas of dark and light. Due to their natural surroundings, it is also common for elephants to have dust and mud on them to stay cool in their hot climates. Consider adding some small variations in color for your elephant's hide. This will help you create a more realistic and dynamic elephant!

Chapter 9:

Clever Fox

Very smart and playful, foxes have become known for their cunning thought processes and are often described in stories as intelligent tricksters.

Foxes exist on almost every continent, with the red fox being the most common of all the many subspecies. Foxes rarely pose a threat to human civilization, thus are seen as lovely and revered creatures. Some people even domesticate and keep foxes as pets. Due to their playful and loyal nature, they can be domesticated relatively easily. However, they are more common in nature versus households and do best this way.

For a large span of history within European countries, foxes were hunted for sport. This became a well-known sport among the higher classes. It was seen as a hard sport, given the cunning nature of foxes. The sport has declined significantly in modern times.

As mentioned above, there are many different variations of foxes throughout the world. In this tutorial we will be focusing on a common red fox. If you are interested, I encourage you to look up some different variations for future projects! You can never have too many different types of needle-felted foxes!

In this project, we will be making a standing fox. I love this figure because it looks very realistic but the standing form gives off a fun and almost cartoonish vibe. When I think of this project, I think of modern stop-motion animation. Check out the tips at the end of this tutorial to find some fun ideas about how to increase the animated style of this little creature.

Fox Instructions

Materials

- Felting wool (white, orange, and black)
- Metal wires
- Felting needle
- Felting pad
- Plastic eyes and nose
- Sharp scissors

Steps

1. First, take white wool and felt a circular ball: this will form the head.

Pro-tip: For this project, it is important that you make sure to firm your ball (head) properly. This will help down the road when you add more color and shape to its head. Remember that foxes have very pointy features. This should take you a bit longer than you may be used to, but do not worry!

2. Now with the same white wool, needle felt an oval cylinder shape for the body. Again, take your time and make sure that this piece is very firm. Since we are not using a wire skeleton for the body, this wool has to stand up on its own. By taking extra time in these beginning steps, you are setting yourself up for success at the end.

3. Join them together with the help of some loose wool. Make sure that the loose wool seals the joining

completely and wraps all around the neck. Also, by layering loose wool around the joining, we are strengthening the figure and smoothing out the base. No lumpy foxes here!

4. Find your sharp scissors and cut to holes for the eyes. Place your plastic eyes into those holes but do not forget to add glue first! Clean up any glue that might have leaked out before it dries. Adding eyes now helps you to determine where various facial features will go.

5. Now grab some orange wool and make the nuzzle. Make sure to check the size against the face before firming it up too much.

6. Attach the muzzle between the eyes.

7. Take some loose orange wool and attach it to the face from the top of the muzzle to the forehead. Make a thicker layer to attach it onto the face. This should be slightly bulky against the small head shape. That is okay: remember that a fox's face is very fluffy!

8. Find some white wool in short strands and attach it to the face on both sides of the muzzle. This will start to shape the pointed fur that foxes are most known for. This will also help blend the muzzle shape into the head better.

9. Take a very thin strand of white wool and attach it to the very tip of the nuzzle—use a very thin needle here. Add thin strands as necessary but remember not to use too much right away.

10. Grab some orange wool and attach it to the area of the eyes. To do this, make sure you have a thin piece and

cover the eyes. When you begin felting the wool, make sure not to hit the eye hiding below. Carefully work the wool around the plastic eye to bring it back out. This section should cover below the eye to the white wool, around the sides of the eye, and well above.

11. Next, we are going to make eyebrows. Foxes are naturally very expressive, so this next step will help you achieve a good expression. Take a thin strip of wool and work it on your pad first to give it some shape. Try not to firm it up too much before you add it onto the head. It should still be loose and long. Use a thin needle here again.

12. Attach the eyebrow directly above the eye. There should be little to no gap between the eyebrow and the eyeball. Felt it into place and trim on the outer eye edge as necessary. The eyebrow should start and stop in a perfect arch right above the eye.

13. Make the bottom eyelid in the exact same technique.

14. Complete the eyebrow and eyelid on both sides. Make sure that they are even or else one eye might look swollen!

15. Grab your orange wool to cover the back of the head. Make sure to tear the wool short then attach it so that you do not have to deal with a piece that is too big for the head. Add layers if necessary.

16. Cover the entire back with orange wool in the same way. Make sure to leave the front belly white and ensure that there is a clean line between the orange and white wool.

17. If desired, take some extra orange wool and add volume to the cheeks. Make sure to stay just at the cheeks to create that pointed fox look. Start small and increase

layers if needed. Be sure to blend the wool in smoothly. Do this on the other side as well to create an even fluff.

18. Now it is time to add some more dimension to the face. Add volume right below the bottom eyelid by layering with wool. Make sure you do not completely cover the eyeball. Add layers as necessary.

19. Now focus on the top of the eye. Add more volume to the top of the eyes just as you did to the bottom. This time, make sure that you are keeping within the arch of the eyebrow that you already established in an earlier step.

20. Find the white wool and tear it very short. Attach it to the white section on the cheek. This will help add volume just as you did with the orange wool and it will add that extra fluff that foxes have. Make sure to add the wool evenly to both sides.

Pro-tip: If you desire, you can take a very small, thin piece of white wool and attach it to the very bottom of the eyeballs. It should not be bulky and should be blended very well. This is not a necessary step but can add some fun dimension to the face.

21. Let us now move on to ears. Make a flat triangular shape in your dark color. Attach white wool to the inside of the triangle and mimic the same shape that you have already established. Make sure that there is a nice border between the dark color and the white wool. Make two and check the size in comparison to the head before you finish the shape.

22. Attach the ears to the top of the head. When attaching the ears, create a slightly concave shape to form a natural ear shape.

Pro-tip: To strengthen the attachment, take some orange wool and add it to the joining area along the back and front of the ears. This will also help blend the ears into the head nicely.

23. Create two small loose balls of white wool and attach them to the bottom of the muzzle. This is to form the mouth and lips of the fox. These balls should blend in evenly with the muzzle, giving just a slight scallop along the edge of the muzzle. Make sure they are even on both sides and make sure that there is a nice line separating them from each other.

24. Attach the nose. Here, I am going to use a plastic nose and attach it in the same way as the eyes. You can use polymer clay if you desire. If you have extra clay noses left over from Isabelle's project, you can use that here. Attach the clay in the same way with a head pin; do not forget to add glass varnish to make a nice shine!

25. Next, grab some white wool to make the lower jaw. This piece should be thick but not too thick that it is out of proportion with the rest of the muzzle. Start small and add as necessary. Do frequent checks with the figure to make sure that the proportions line up well. The lower jaw should fit in the area below the lips that we just created. It should rest just within those top lips and should not be bigger than that area. In a realistic figure, the top lips should look like they slightly cover the side of the lower jaw. Make sure there is a distinct line between the lower jaw and upper lips.

26. Add some dimension to the face by outlining the mouth. You can use thin strips of black wool for continuity but black acrylic paint also works to outline the shape of the mouth. Whichever method you choose, follow the

established lines of the mouth and make sure the lines are not too large. Add some black color to the top of the nose to blend the color between the black button nose and the orange muzzle. If you are using wool, use very thin strands to achieve this look. If you are using paint, blend the paint from the nose to out on the muzzle.

27. Onto the legs and hands.

28. For the legs, take your wire and twist it evenly to strengthen it. Grab some orange wool and wrap it tightly around the wire. Roll the wool around the wire until you achieve your desired thickness. Then, take your needle and poke it until it firms up around the wire. Find your black wool and add it to the bottom tip of the leg. Blend the black wool in well.

29. Make two legs of equal length and repeat the same process for the hands. Make sure that the hands are ever so slightly shorter than the legs.

30. Attach the legs to the side of the body. Add more layers of orange wool to strengthen the attachment and smooth out the surface just as you did for other attachments. By adding layers here, you are also helping form the natural shape of the hind legs which tends to be thicker on real animals.

31. Onto the tail.

32. The tail is created in a similar way that the legs are formed. Take a wire and wrap it evenly, firmly wrapping white wool around it. Add more layers to add the natural fluffy shape of the fox's tail. Then, felt the wool to firm it up. Find orange wool and add it to the tail on the top section where it will be attached to the body. This will

leave a white tip at the bottom. Make sure that the orange wool is much fluffier than the white wool to create that natural shape.

Pro-tip: Add thin layers of black wool to the orange section of the tail to create a dynamic color. This is not a necessary step but it helps to pull in the darker ears and the black of the facial features.

33. Join the tail at the backside of the body of the fox. Add layers of orange wool to strengthen the attachment and to add fluff to the backside of the fox. This will also help you blend the tail to the body and create a natural smooth shape. Make sure that you add layers of wool to all sides of the tail attachment. This will help make it even.

34. Take orange wool and add significant volume around the tail and legs on the body. This fox figure should have curvy hips and this area should be rounder than the top torso. Keep poking until the additional fur is smooth and firm.

35. Attach the arms in the same way as the legs by adding layers of wool to strengthen the attachment, blend the arms to the body, and smooth out the figure. Unlike the legs, you should be using thin layers of wool here because the arms should not have as much bulk as the legs. Make sure your layers cover all sides of the arm attachment. Keep layering with more thin wool as needed.

Your fox is ready to frolic through some fields!

Pro-tip:

Since we have created a unique, standing fox, this is a great opportunity to make it like a realistic cartoon character. You can do this by adding accessories to the fox. The best and easiest accessory is a lovely little scarf. Choose your favorite color or choose a color that you think the fox would like best and create a long scarf wrapping around the neck of the fox. If you are feeling adventurous, try out mittens or maybe even a lovely turtleneck sweater!

Alternatively, you can experiment with different colors/species of foxes. Think white for an arctic fox, or you can alter this design to make it more subdued and brown. You can either do this by following the above instructions exactly, but layer thin strands of black wool over the orange to create dimension within the color. Or you can start by using a more reddish-brown color (think like a rusty red or orange that closely resembles brown). Do some image searches to see what colors are available.

You can also create a fluffier fox by following the above instructions. When you come to the end of the project, take your needle and gently comb the wool in the natural direction that fur would grow, which is down. You can do this to all areas of the figure apart from the muzzle and the lower jaw. If you do this, be sure to trim some of the overhanging wool that you pulled away from the figure. You want your fox to be fluffy but neat.

Wrapping Things Up

If you are reading this closing chapter, that means you just completed your intermediate guide to needle felting. Take a moment to pat yourself on the back! You did it! Now you have two full needle felting guides under your belt. May we say what a pro you have become?

Here we are, at the end of the intermediate guide to needle felting. Man, has it been a fun ride. I hope that it has been as fun for you as it has been for me. I also hope that you are loving all of the little creatures you just made.

I also hope that you are immensely proud of all the hard work that you put in to get to where you are right now. You would not be here if you never carved out specific time in your weeks to work on improving your needle felting skills.

I had such a fun time putting together the beginner and intermediate guides for you, and it fills my heart with so much joy that you took the time out of your busy schedule to sit down with me and learn the unique art of needle felting. While I may not know what led you here, I am so happy that you showed up and kept showing up. That shows dedication and makes you truly noble. Shall we start the knighting ceremony now?

Take a moment to pause and think about what created the spark that led you to want to learn how to needle felt. Was it a friend or family member? Did you see a perfectly adorable little needle felted creature online? Maybe you were gifted a needle felting kit by someone who thought you might like it. Take a moment to just consider what it was that brought you to pick up the art. If a person that you know got you interested in needle felting, maybe consider taking a few minutes to thank them for that. If they are a fellow feltie, invite them to grab coffee and talk about needle felting. Talk about what you most love about needle felting, talk about what you have most struggled with, and of course be sure to share photos with them of all the amazing little creatures that you have made. Chances are, you will probably find that you two share some of the same love and frustrations that are involved in this art form!

These guides were such a labor of love for me and were such a joy to put together. Please know that at every step of the way, I have been silently cheering you on as you flip from page to page. I hope that you felt a little bit of connection to me through my guides and that you feel like you almost got to know me a little bit, too. Writing this now, I feel like I am getting to know you, too! The art of needle felting is something that brings me great joy in my personal life. In creating these two little guides, I wanted to share that love and share what I have learned in my journey through learning needle felting with the hope that you can take something away from the advice I included in these guides. I also hope that both of these guides have fueled a creative fire and that you will keep stoking that fire as you make your way through new projects. As I am sure you know by now, the art of needle felting is extremely addictive. This is one addiction that you will not want to quit!

My main hope for you reading this guide is that you come away from this book more confident in your needle felting ability. Is there still more to learn? Sure! Like I said before, there is always something new to learn in this art form and that is what makes it so special.

Take a moment to celebrate how far you have come in just two short books. Look back on the very first shape that you created: a heart. Looking back on it now, you probably are shocked by how simple it is to make a heart. That shows you how much you have learned! If you have a few moments, go back and make a new heart. You can make it in the same color or material as your very first heart or something different: the choice is yours. When you finish making the new heart, set it next to your very first heart. Take a moment to notice any differences in your experience from the very beginning to now. Did you make the new heart faster? Is your new heart smoother? Does it have a more definable shape? Chances are, you will notice some difference. Revel in this difference. Revel in your improvement. You have come so far!

Together, we have started off with simple flat shapes and built up our structure skills. We learned how to make pin cushions, funky garlands (I still love that macaron garland so very much, and I hope you do, too!), and we began to take our first steps toward creating animal shapes. In this intermediate guide, we really stepped up our game. In this book, we used quite a few wire skeletons or armatures which are such a great way to start out a needle felting project. Wire skeletons not only help you create very detailed and varied shapes, they also allow you to create movable structures. Even after felting, the wire can be bent to give your figures new poses and shapes. How cool is that?

Beyond that, we learned how to use some brand new tools like the multi-needle holder and the Zullitool. Both tools are great to have within your armory and will be extremely useful as you continue on this needle felting journey.

In this intermediate guide, we also learned some very important tips, tricks, and advice. I hope you found some new tips and tricks to put into your needle felting tool bag. I also hope that those little nuggets of advice inspire you to seek out more information. With a growing community of needle felters out there, there is literally an endless amount of information available to you. I strongly encourage you to seek out like-minded individuals within the felting community. This could be online through blogs or videos or in person.

Maybe this journey has also inspired you to build your own community. Have you thought about starting your own blog to track your needle felting journey? At least think it over for a little bit. This could be a great way to meet new people and find more felties out there. Who knows, maybe you might even inspire a beginner who is struggling to find their groove. Think back to when you started out in the beginner's guide. What skills and techniques did you struggle with at first? Was there any information that you wished you knew before you jumped into your first project? Even think about when you made the switch from the beginner's guide to the intermediate guide.

There was a pretty big jump there. What were you most intimidated by? What techniques did you find that you had to practice over and over again? Take a moment to think about all of these things. Not only does it give you a pretty good idea about how much you have learned and how much hard work you went through to get here: these questions are not unique to just you. Chances are, there are lots of beginners just starting out and asking these same questions. You have the unique opportunity to become a leader and mentor to someone just starting out. Reach out: I am sure you will be awfully glad when you do!

If the online community does not really feel like your thing, consider creating your own in-person community. Start off with one or two friends or some colleagues. Find someone whose interest is sparked when you share your passion for needle felting and help them get started. Now that you know so much, you can be there for beginners to help them along their path. Encourage and uplift them, help them by answering their questions or maybe even supplying them with their very first needle. Needle felting is so much more fun when it is done with others. Find your posse. They will be there with you through *stick* and thin. Because people who felt together, stay together.

Now all that is left to do is to name all of your animals and animals variations. To me, this is such a fun little moment to really take ownership of your creations. Plus, when you are showing off your incredible needle felting skills to your adoring fans, you can introduce each little figure by name.

References

Anh, N. (2019). Elephant Walking. In *Unsplash*. https://unsplash.com/photos/QJbyG6Ooick

Binc Bonc. (2018a). Fox Needle Felting Tutorial [YouTube Video]. In *YouTube*. https://www.youtube.com/watch?v=-uc95YaHF50&feature=youtu.be

Binc Bonc. (2018b). Teddy Bear Needle Felting Tutorial [YouTube Video]. In *YouTube*. https://www.youtube.com/watch?v=lgZEcxdH4MI&feature=youtu.be

Constable, C. (2018, November 16). *Advanced Needle Felting Projects for Experienced Enthusiasts*. WonderfulDIY. https://wonderfuldiy.com/advanced-needle-felting-projects/

Dinata, Y. (2018). Black mouse. In *Unsplash*. https://unsplash.com/photos/k9NVUS7PS4A

How to Needle Felt. (n.d.). WikiHow. Retrieved November 8, 2020, from https://www.wikihow.com/Needle-Felt

Huaman, C. R. (2018). Alpaca standing on brown soil. In *Unsplash*. https://unsplash.com/photos/gdBqSojOV38

Kurfess, S. (2020). Blue nintendo switch game. In *Unsplash*. https://unsplash.com/photos/hzad7011p5I

Lyashenko, O. (2019). Teddy Bear. In *Unsplash*. https://unsplash.com/photos/7XoKI25ufno

McCutcheon, S. (2018). Free Love. In Unsplash. https://unsplash.com/photos/d55BPRk0dnk/info

Potgieter, A. (2020). Brown lion lying down. In *Unsplash*. https://unsplash.com/photos/GV2LxPJArgQ

Sandbakk, L. (2016). Brown Fox. In *Unsplash*. https://unsplash.com/photos/HQqIOc8oYro

St-Hilaline Poulin, M. (2019). White animal. In *Unsplash*. https://unsplash.com/photos/PSxIoipDUZ4

Tahoe. (2019). Grey and White Wolf. In *Unsplash*. https://unsplash.com/photos/Eaz0wqnV1VQ

Top 25 Needle Felting Tips and Tricks. (n.d.). Kawaii Felting. Retrieved November 8, 2020, from https://kawaiifelting.com/about/sample-page/my-top-25-needle-felting-tips-and-tricks/

Lightning Source UK Ltd.
Milton Keynes UK
UKHW021015171122
412356UK00011B/1333